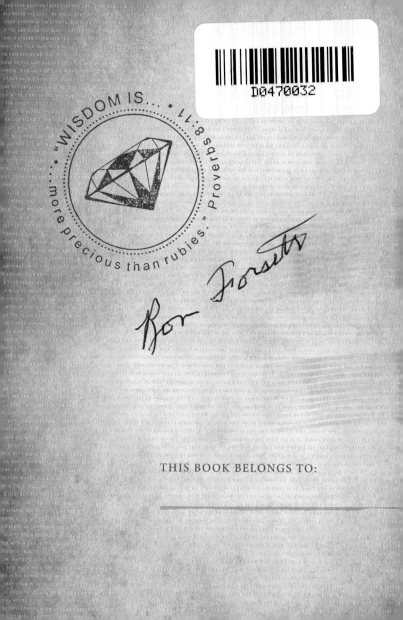

"WISDOM IS...

...more precious than rubies." Proverbs 8:11

Ron Forsett

THIS BOOK BELONGS TO:

We all need wisdom—but where can we find insights that lead us deeper into our relationship with God? Dan and Ron come to the rescue with *The Wisdom Challenge*, a terrific resource that sets forth a sustainable path for pursuing and growing in God's wisdom for a lifetime. If you want a heart of wisdom, *The Wisdom Challenge* is for you!

LEE STROBEL

New York Times best-selling author
Founding director, The Lee Strobel Center for Evangelism and Applied Apologetics at Colorado Christian University

THE
WISDOM
CHALLENGE

Experience the
life-changing
power of Proverbs

Dan Britton & Ron Forseth

BroadStreet
PUBLISHING

BroadStreet Publishing® Group, LLC

Savage, Minnesota, USA

BroadStreetPublishing.com

The Wisdom Challenge

978-1-4245-6083-7 (faux leather)

978-1-4245-6084-4 (eBook)

Stock or custom editions of BroadStreet Publishing titles may be purchased in bulk for educational, business, ministry, fundraising, or sales promotional use. For information, please email orders@broadstreetpublishing.com.

Cover and interior by Garborg Design at GarborgDesign.com

Printed in China

21 22 23 24 25 5 4 3 2 1

DEDICATION

We would like to dedicate this book
to our Proverbs Partners who have
joined us in the pursuit of wisdom.

ACKNOWLEDGMENTS

We would like to humbly acknowledge the stellar support we've received from the BroadStreet team in getting this book to press. Special thanks to Carlton Garborg for your leadership and for literally joining us in *The Wisdom Challenge*; to Tim Payne, Michelle Winger, Rachel Libke, Nina Derek, Chris Garborg, and so many others working behind the scenes. We are grateful for your grace, patience, and encouragement. Without you, *The Wisdom Challenge* would still just be an idea.

Deep appreciation to our editor, Danielle Ripley-Burgess, for bringing so much energy to the process and for taking our writing to the next level. Thanks for jumping in and making this book become a reality. You made it come alive, and we will be forever grateful! A big thank you to Kallie Muck and Claire Matera who made this book better with one last rigorous edit.

I, Dan, would like to thank my family who have all joined me in *The Wisdom Challenge*: Dawn, Kallie, Austin, Abigail, Garrett, Elijah, and Claire. Mom and Dad, you modeled godly wisdom every day for me and always pointed me to the Word of God. Additionally, I am grateful for my FCA teammates who journeyed with me through Proverbs to get wisdom, discernment, and understanding. Thanks Andriy, Jin, Mark, Kellen, Silas, Steve, Andrew, Craig, Holt, Scott, Janet, and many others!

I, Ron, would like to thank my wife, Carol, my daughter, Rachel, and my son, Randy, for supporting me in my pursuit of wisdom, and especially for joining me so often as Proverbs Partners. My father, Fred Forseth, has exhibited profound wisdom for a lifetime as did my mother, Jean Forseth, who listened to the Bible daily from her sickbed for twenty-three years and eagerly shared with me and my six siblings her love for biblical wisdom. Thanks, too, to Eric Ely for first quoting Proverbs to me over forty years ago and challenging me to pursue wisdom.

CONTENTS

Foreword   9

The Wisdom Challenge   11

CHAPTER 1 Wisdom's Impact   13

CHAPTER 2 Wisdom's Promise   25

CHAPTER 3 Wisdom's Invitation   36

CHAPTER 4 Wisdom's Gift   49

CHAPTER 5 Wisdom's Tree   57

CHAPTER 6 Wisdom's Legacy   68

CHAPTER 7 Wisdom's Journey   77

Author Bios   140

Next Steps   144

FOREWORD

Dan and Ron are not the creators of wisdom, and they both make that clear. Wisdom comes from God; He is the true source. However, Dan and Ron have been charged with a message from God to uncover and declare God's heart for wisdom—and to encourage everyone who wants it to seek and discover it.

Today our world loves riches; silver, gold, and rubies hold much value. But Proverbs says wisdom is even more valuable than all of these. That's why I love this book. Our generation needs wisdom and *The Wisdom Challenge* will remind you of its value and help you discover it.

Whether you're brand new to the Bible or you've studied it for years, doing *The Wisdom Challenge* is something we all need and can benefit from. Deep down, we all want wisdom. We're made in the image of God, and God is the source of wisdom. We all want to make a positive impact. *The Wisdom Challenge* is a great resource to give us the wisdom we need to make a greater impact in the world.

Through *The Wisdom Challenge*, you'll gain advice on relationships, money, leadership, and spirituality. You'll read about a just God, a merciful God, a loving God, and a holy God. In Proverbs, we're encouraged to hold our tongues, to rule our spirits, to guard our hearts, and to give great gifts. It's powerful, practical, and applicable.

I hope you will join me on this incredible journey and take *The Wisdom Challenge* for yourself and for your relationship with God, the One who wants to give wisdom to us all. The pursuit of wisdom is worth it, and receiving it is an incredible blessing.

> Blessed are those who listen to me,
>> watching daily at my doors,
>> waiting at my doorway.
> For those who find me find life
>> and receive favor from the Lord.

PROVERBS 8:34–35 NIV

God bless,

JON GORDON

Bestselling author of *The Carpenter* and *The Garden*

THE
WISDOM
CHALLENGE

Pursue

Read Proverbs every day to pursue wisdom.

Partner

Invite a Proverbs Partner to read the same chapter of Proverbs, and through a text, email, or quick phone call, share a brief reflection about what verse or insight impacted you.

Pass It On

Challenge your Proverbs Partner to invite someone else to take *The Wisdom Challenge* with him or her at the start of the next month.

Chapter 1

WISDOM'S IMPACT

Walk with the wise and become wise.

PROVERBS 13:20 NIV

Have you ever felt that your heart was as dry as a dirt clod, like a brittle tree with parched roots long deprived of water? Have you ever longed to hear from God, wondering where He might be? I have. It's rare for me to hear so clearly from God, but on March 1, 2012, I had an exception. That day I discovered that not only did He care for me in a rather personal way, but in that desert, He had also prepared a surprise that would alter the course of my life.

For whatever reason, over the previous decade, my dynamic connection with God had shriveled up to the point I began to wonder where He had gone or if He even really cared about me. I remember being at our home in North San Diego county, sitting in the comfy recliner in the early morning before anyone else in the family was up. I was a bit down emotionally but regrettably had come to accept that as the norm. That was soon to change. The conversation went like this:

God, what can I do to reconnect with You? I asked silently.

He answered, unmistakably, *Each day eat spiritual food before you eat physical food.*

Okay. That's simple enough. So, You want me to read the Bible before I eat breakfast? I answered.

He replied, *Exactly.*

Where do I start? I asked.

He answered quite simply, *Proverbs.*

And that was the beginning.

I was glad God didn't ignore my question and especially glad for the nudge to take the first step in a specific direction. That morning, reaching for my leather-bound Bible, I went straight into the book of Proverbs and, unexpectedly, enjoyed it more than the best breakfast I could have eaten from an award-winning chef. It was rich, alive, and delicious. It felt as if the pages radiated an energy I hadn't experienced in a very long time.

> The proverbs of Solomon son of David,
>> king of Israel:
> for gaining wisdom and instruction;
>> for understanding words of insight;
> for receiving instruction in prudent behavior,
>> doing what is right and just and fair;
> for giving prudence to those who are simple,
>> knowledge and discretion to the young—
> let the wise listen and add to their learning,

and let the discerning get guidance—
for understanding proverbs and parables,
the sayings and riddles of the wise.

PROVERBS 1:1–6 NIV

The words quenched my soul as God Himself brought verse after verse into vivid focus. God was clearly present. Each line I read breathed fresh life into my heart. It was as if my soul were coming out of a long, cold winter. This thing called wisdom was beginning to grip me as some sort of obsession. My appetite for it was rising up and driving me forward.

I believe God was smiling, that He looked over my shoulder and carefully released insight and understanding as I read the sentences one after the other. From the beginning of my brief conversation with God to the time I finished the first chapter of Proverbs, it must have been only about ten minutes. But when it was over, my soul was filled up like I'd just consumed a buffet, and I was ready for whatever the day had for me. I can't remember what I had for breakfast that day, but that encounter with God remains vivid in my mind these many years later. Those ten minutes changed my life.

I repeated this exercise the next day. And the day after that. Each day the same thing happened, all the way to the end of the month. I was spiritually hungry, and Proverbs fed me. At the beginning of each month, I desired to keep going. I'd begin with the first chapter of Proverbs, reading the chapter that matched the month's date. With most months having thirty-one days and Proverbs having thirty-one chapters, it was easy to stay on track.

Three months into my personal wisdom journey, I had another nudge from God and sensed He wanted me to walk this wisdom journey with someone else. I wasn't to keep this for myself; God wanted to multiply it! He was forming *The Wisdom Challenge*. It wasn't to be my own personal exercise but rather a movement that would spark a thirst for wisdom and feed a spiritual hunger among thousands all over the world.

God put my friend Dan, at the Fellowship of Christian Athletes, on my heart. Dan is a kind, God-loving man with a heap of wisdom already, and he has a dynamic leadership role in a global ministry. Our friendship had been an ongoing source of encouragement for about ten years, and I sensed Dan was the person God wanted me to invite into my wisdom journey. I called him and shared about my month-long encounter with God. Then I invited him to take *The Wisdom Challenge* with me. He accepted.

Walking *with* Another

I had spent time with Ron for several years, and as our relationship grew, we were spiritually sharpening one another on a regular basis. I loved how he would always go out of his way to care for those he encountered, especially the "least of these." He carries a special awareness for the people most others ignore or don't take the time to help. I was stretched in my faith when I spent time with Ron. It was always good to hear from him. When I got Ron's call, he shared that he wanted to read the book of Proverbs with me for the upcoming month.

"Would you like to be my partner to go through Proverbs

with me?" Ron asked. I jumped on it! Ron was getting ready to stretch me once again, and so was God.

I already had a regular morning devotional time, so when Ron explained *The Wisdom Challenge*, I just added another ten minutes each day. It seemed simple enough. In the past, I had taken on some Proverbs challenges where I read a chapter of Proverbs each day for thirty-one days and greatly benefited from this exercise; however, I had never done it *with* someone. I was ready to experience something new.

Ron and I decided to both read the same chapter of Proverbs (the one that matched the date), and then we would text each other what God revealed to us. We encouraged and commented on one another's insights. After only a few days, I was blown away.

The big surprise wasn't necessarily what I was gleaning from Proverbs but the dynamic interaction with Ron through a couple texts each morning. It made our insights from Proverbs come alive. It gave them substance and application. And accountability! The interaction was life-giving. Each morning I couldn't wait to see what God would show me in Proverbs and share it with Ron. Additionally, my excitement would grow reading what Ron discovered. I found myself eager each morning to know:

Will his inspiration come from the same verse as mine?

What will God reveal to my friend this morning?

How can I encourage Ron in his walk?

How will Ron challenge me?

For thirty-one days, Ron and I texted at least once each morning for *The Wisdom Challenge*. It was a powerful month of revelation, understanding, and growth. As Paul writes in Ephesians 1:18–19, the eyes of my heart were opened. Each day was a double portion of learning—my own insight and Ron's. Throughout the day, I was compelled and convicted to live out what I shared with Ron because I was motivated to apply the wisdom I had gleaned. This was a game changer.

Toward the middle of our month, Ron challenged me to begin thinking of someone I could invite to do *The Wisdom Challenge* with me at the start of the next month. I immediately accepted. I couldn't wait to share this exercise with others. My mind swirled as I thought of all the people who would benefit from doing it. It felt like I possessed a special gift that could bless another person for an entire month. So the following month, I carried it on. I decided to start with my son, Elijah. Spending thirty-one straight days in God's Word with my son and hearing how God was speaking to him was a gift from God—something I will never forget!

Growing Together

Once we finished our month in Proverbs together, we each started *The Wisdom Challenge* with someone else. Although technically reading the same Scripture passages each month, Proverbs still felt so new. Taking the challenge with others brought new insights. New principles. New lessons. New takeaways.

Over the years, we have journeyed with countless friends, coworkers, and family members through Proverbs. The crazy thing is that it often feels like we're going through Proverbs for the first time again.

Ron has walked through Proverbs with at least one new person each month for over one hundred months. Dan has also taken the challenge with many friends and family members. Through his teammates at the Fellowship of Christian Athletes, he's seen it take off around the world. Numerous international leaders in dozens of countries are doing this simple discipline. Men and women around the world are growing in wisdom. And it's changing lives!

What's Your Impact?

What kind of impact do you want to make in life? Have you ever thought about that? Everyone desires to make an impact. The question is never, "Do you want to make an impact?" but rather, "What kind of impact do you hope to make?"

Bonnie and Clyde, Jack the Ripper, and Joseph Stalin all left legacies, but their names are forever remembered with regret. Jesse Owens, Abraham Lincoln, and Mother Teresa also left legacies, and the world will forever remember them for the extraordinary impact they made. We'd venture to say you want to make a positive impact. That's why you're reading a book about wisdom, which will help you make that impact. How? A key is found in Proverbs 13:20 where it talks about walking with the wise to become wise.

If we want to make a difference, we need to become wise, and a key way to become wise is to pursue wisdom *with* others. That is why *The Wisdom Challenge* isn't for you alone; it's for you and the other people you invite to join you on the journey. We cannot isolate ourselves and expect to become wise. Wisdom always comes in the context of relationships.

Wisdom + relationships = impact.

Wisdom - relationships = nothing.

Wisdom by itself is useless. True wisdom comes in the context of relationships, first with God and then with others. Walking *with* the wise leads to wisdom. Walking without the wise leads to trouble.

Walk with the wise and become wise;
associate with fools and get in trouble.

PROVERBS 13:20 NLT

The power of *with* is the key. We've found that walking *with* each other through *The Wisdom Challenge* has changed our lives, and we believe it will change yours too.

The Wisdom Challenge has taught me to lead with practical application from the book of Proverbs while getting closer to others. In nine months, I have partnered with fifteen people as we walked in wisdom together. And now they are walking with others!

ANDRIY, PROVERBS PARTNER

Chapter 2

WISDOM'S PROMISE

God gave Solomon wisdom and very great insight,
and a breadth of understanding
as measureless as the sand on the seashore.
1 Kings 4:29 niv

Are you sold on pursuing wisdom? Do you know the best place to find it? Wisdom is a promise that comes from God. But that's not all. Wisdom carries a promise. If you believe this promise, apply this promise, and live this promise, your life will be marked with mission and meaning. You will experience God's power and purpose. Those around you will also be marked. What is this promise wisdom carries? It's four simple words: *Nothing compares with wisdom.*

Sometimes we refer to this as "The Nothing Promise" because nothing you get in life is more valuable than wisdom. Wisdom trumps *everything*. Proverbs makes this promise in chapter 3 and repeats it in chapter 8:

> Wisdom is more precious than rubies,
>   and nothing you desire can compare with her.

PROVERBS 8:11 NIV

Wisdom is *the* primary ingredient for success in life. Without it, failure is guaranteed. With wisdom comes success and impact, something we all desire.

Wisdom Is Counter-Cultural

A survey[1] asked seven hundred people, "If you could say in one word what you want more of in life, what would that be?"

---

1   https://www.linkedin.com/pulse/top-10-things-people-want-life-cant-figure-out-how-get-kathy-caprino/

Here were the top ten responses:

1. Happiness
2. Money
3. Freedom
4. Peace
5. Joy
6. Balance
7. Fulfillment
8. Confidence
9. Stability
10. Passion

No surprises. This is most definitely what our culture desires. And truth be told, most of *us* would have mentioned several of these answers in our top ten lists, too, had we been asked to take the survey. However, we noticed there is one response that didn't make the list: wisdom. Yet when we seek wisdom, everything else falls into place.

If people understood the value and promise of wisdom, it would be at the top of their lists. After years of doing *The Wisdom Challenge*, wisdom is number one on our list. Why?

Because of wisdom's promise—which comes straight from the Bible.

Solomon's Wisdom

Solomon, who was born about 990 years before Jesus, was the third king of the nation of Israel. He took the throne at age nineteen and ruled for forty years until he died at age fifty-nine. Solomon's father was King David who, from an early age, challenged Solomon to pursue wisdom with all of his heart. When Solomon took the throne, God made him an incredible offer—an offer all of us would like. God said to Solomon, "Ask for whatever you want me to give you" (2 Chronicles 1:7 NIV).

Learning from his father, David, Solomon knew just what he wanted. He responded, "Give me wisdom and knowledge, that I may lead this people, for who is able to govern this great people of yours?" (v. 10). God loved Solomon's request. This is how He responded: "Since this is your heart's desire and you have not asked for wealth, possessions or honor, nor for the death of your enemies, and since you have not asked for a long life but for wisdom and knowledge to govern my people over whom I have made you king, therefore wisdom and knowledge will be given you. And I will also give you wealth, possessions and honor, such as no king who was before you ever had and none after you will have" (2 Chronicles 1:11–12 NIV).

Solomon's wise request for wisdom set him on a path to a rather impressive life. Here are a few highlights of Solomon's life, a life that was marked with wisdom:

- Solomon was able to restore a stolen baby to his birth mother by suggesting the baby be cut in half.
- Solomon's wisdom exceeded the wisdom of all the wisemen of the east.
- Solomon spoke three thousand proverbs, of which less than one-third are found in the book of Proverbs.
- Solomon became an expert biologist and botanist, learning secrets of wisdom from creation.
- All the kings and queens of the earth sought wisdom from Solomon.

Obviously the one word that best describes Solomon is *wise*. Solomon experienced the value of obtaining wisdom. He wrote in Proverbs 3:15 and again in Proverbs 8:11 that *nothing* compares to wisdom. What's wonderful for us is that he didn't keep it to himself. Wisdom led him to share it.

The Book of Proverbs

God granted Solomon the wisdom and knowledge he asked for, and Solomon took note of what God showed him. Much of the wisdom Solomon received can now be found in the book of Proverbs. Wisdom is found throughout Scripture, but Proverbs is a one-stop place to find it. It's no surprise that when God invited us into a wisdom journey, He had us start in Proverbs. The book is like a hill with thousands of gems of wise insight embedded within. If you want wisdom and you want to discover its promise, Proverbs is where to start. This is where we can get out our picks and shovels to start digging for treasure.

All throughout the Proverbs, Solomon unpacks and writes about the wisdom he received so people like you and me can receive it too. Through Solomon's writings, we not only see that nothing compares with wisdom, but we also see the promise it carries. Here are just a few of the assets Solomon says accompany wisdom:

- Glory
- Knowledge
- Insight
- Understanding
- Riches
- Prosperity
- Honor
- Contentment
- Confidence
- Good health
- Divine protection
- Long life
- Peace
- Favor
- Knowledge of God Himself

Wisdom is simply incredible. Here's an amazing thing: God is eager to give us wisdom and bless our lives beyond our imagination too. This blessing is ours for the taking as we grab hold of wisdom and don't let go!

The End Prize

Wisdom brings many things our hearts desire—much of what we find on popular top ten lists. But there's one promise tucked inside God's wisdom that beats all others: the knowledge of God Himself. This is the end prize, the ultimate promise, of wisdom. Jesus, who knew the book of Proverbs from beginning to end, said this: "Now this is eternal life: that they know you, the only true God, and Jesus Christ, whom you have sent" (John 17:3 NIV).

True wisdom from God will lead to us knowing God and entering into an eternal relationship with Him that goes beyond what we can imagine. The wisdom in Proverbs can bless and benefit *anyone*, but for those who have a relationship with God, wisdom transforms *all* aspects and dimensions of life—body, mind, and spirit.

No eye has seen, no ear has heard, and no mind
has imagined what God has prepared for those
who love him.

1 Corinthians 2:9 nlt

You see, wisdom from God reveals that the wisest thing we can do with our lives is run into the arms of our loving Creator. How do we do this? We believe and trust in Jesus. We turn from our wrongdoing and ask God to live in our hearts. When we approach God with a humble heart and accept His grace and mercy for ourselves, we are restored to God and ushered into an unending relationship with Him that lasts forever. As a free gift, we receive the ultimate wisdom, Jesus Christ, and every promise from God, as described in 1 Corinthians: "It is because of him that you are in Christ Jesus, who has become for us wisdom from God—that is, our righteousness, holiness and redemption" (1 Corinthians 1:30 niv).

Wisdom is from God, and wisdom brings us unity with God through a relationship with Jesus. If you have never accepted this gift of salvation, will you stop and ask for it right now? You can receive it by expressing your faith in Christ like this:

> *Heavenly Father, I accept Your free gift of salvation today. Thank You for sending Your Son, Jesus, to die on the cross for my sin so that I can be forgiven. Please forgive me of all my sins. Right now I declare that Jesus Christ is Lord and believe that You raised Him from the dead. I receive Your gift of forgiveness and life through Your Son, Jesus. I trust You and I give You my life. Thank You for Your amazing gift of salvation. Amen.*

A Powerful Invitation

If you prayed that prayer for the first time just now, *congratulations*! Be sure to tell someone; it's the most powerful prayer you'll ever pray. The wisest one too. When you live with the wisdom of Christ in your life, you'll experience wisdom's promises. You'll also be able to discern wisdom's invitation.

The daily time focused on this book unlocked a love of the Word in me like never before. It was also wonderful to see the power of wisdom infuse my life, not just while reading this during the thirty-one-day journey but also continuing long after.

KIM, PROVERBS PARTNER

Chapter 3

WISDOM'S INVITATION

*The fear of the L*ORD *is the beginning of wisdom;*
all who follow his precepts have good understanding.
To him belongs eternal praise.

PSALM 111:10 NIV

World history is full of gold discoveries and gold rushes that followed. Miners would leave all they had behind—family, friends, houses, jobs, and more—for a chance at striking it rich and finding gold. If they were lucky enough to find it, it made them wealthy beyond imagination. Stories of people going from rags to riches made gold rushes a common occurance throughout the nineteenth century. Just look at some of the greatest pursuits of wealth during that time:

- The San Francisco Gold Rush of 1849
- The Victoria, Australia, Gold Rush of 1851
- The Otago, New Zealand, Gold Rush of 1861
- The Witwatersrand, South Africa, Gold Rush of 1886
- The Canadian Klondike Gold Rush of 1896

Today we still see remnants and tell stories of times when people rushed to mine for gold. But what if we rushed to mine for something even more valuable than gold? What if we realized wisdom offers us an even more powerful invitation and riches beyond belief? Maybe there would have been more "wisdom rushes" than gold rushes. Can you imagine?

Nothing Compares

The Bible compares the value of wisdom to riches and jewels. Wisdom is what brings ultimate, long-lasting wealth. With great earnest, Proverbs invites us to pursue and receive wisdom. It wants us to rush to the Word of God and search for wisdom. Check out Solomon's alluring invitation in chapter 3:

Blessed are those who find wisdom,
> those who gain understanding,
for she is more profitable than silver
> and yields better returns than gold.
She is more precious than rubies;
> nothing you desire can compare with her.
Long life is in her right hand;
> in her left hand are riches and honor.
Her ways are pleasant ways,
> and all her paths are peace.
She is a tree of life to those who take hold of her;
> those who hold her fast will be blessed.

PROVERBS 3:13–18 NIV

Wisdom is more profitable than silver and gold. Better than a finely polished 10-carat diamond. Better than a sack full of unblemished rubies. Wow, now that's valuable!

More than Rubies

It's easy for us to understand the value of gold and diamonds, and we know gold is more valuable than silver. But did you know rubies are more valuable than gold?

> Wisdom is more precious than rubies,
>> and nothing you desire can compare with her.

PROVERBS 8:11 NIV

How much is a ruby worth? According to the International Gem Society, in 2015, a ruby that weighed more than 25 carats sold for more than $1 million a carat—$30 million dollars! By comparison, a 50-carat diamond offered by Christie's sold for under $10 million—only about $200,000 per carat.

Rubies or diamonds? Pick wisdom!

A half cup of sizeable rubies could be worth in excess of a billion dollars! And wisdom is worth more than rubies. Nothing can compare with wisdom. Nothing! Why all this comparing? To incite us to push the pursuit of wisdom to the top of our priorities.

Wisdom is worth more than massive amounts of money. It's worth more than our combined net worth. Wisdom is worth more than what we could earn from our first paycheck to the last paycheck of our lives. It's even worth more than all of the combined estates of Bill Gates and Jeff Bezos—which means if you get it, you'll be richer than the richest people on earth. No exaggeration. God says wisdom is *that* valuable!

Finding Wisdom

Once we grasp how valuable wisdom is, we start asking the right questions. Namely, "How can I get wisdom?" The astounding thing is that all throughout Proverbs, we see wisdom as an invitation from God.

James tells us more about how to get wisdom: "If any of you lacks wisdom, you should ask God, who gives generously to all without finding fault, and it will be given to you" (James 1:5 NIV). We get wisdom by asking for it. God has invited us to request it from Him, just like Solomon did. As we ask for wisdom, we will see its starting line: the fear of the Lord. Solomon, in all of his wisdom, was emphatic about telling us where wisdom begins. Solomon knew you can't have wisdom and not fear the Lord:

The fear of the LORD is the beginning of wisdom,

and knowledge of the Holy One is understanding.

PROVERBS 9:10 NIV

For many, fearing the Lord may generate negative images of fire falling from heaven or a vengeful God getting ready to punish and judge. This terrifying imagery leads some to say fearing God simply means "reverence, respect, or honor for the Lord." Others who envision God in this way often shut Him out altogether with the thought, *If God is so mean and terrifying, I don't want anything to do with him.* But this response is incredibly sad, and it comes from a misunderstanding of who God really is. This picture of God lacks wisdom.

We want to help explain what God has shown us about fearing the Lord. It's important that we do not diminish this powerful phrase: fearing the Lord. If we do, we will miss the richness of the fear God is talking about. An accurate understanding can bring powerful meaning to our lives.

God is not a cosmic killjoy who somehow delights in terrorizing people. A true understanding of "the fear of the

Lord" starts with understanding the nature of God, specifically two of His attributes: *God is holy* and *God is love*.

Holy means God hates evil—He won't tolerate it.

Love means God wants our best—He went to great lengths to provide it.

It's not either/or; it's both. God is holy *and* love. The cross of Jesus demonstrates this. Jesus died to defeat evil because He loved us. In the cross we see holiness and love perfectly harmonized. Understanding how God can be both holy and love will create a fear of the Lord in us. When that happens, it's an exceptional, beautiful, and powerful thing. When we rightly see God, it produces and protects our relationship with Him, and it draws us *to* Him rather than driving us away.

Here's an example to help explain the fear of the Lord. Let's say a father and his seven-year-old daughter are playing catch on the front lawn. They toss the ball back and forth. On one throw, the daughter can't make the catch, and the ball soars past her and bounces into the street. At the same time, a truck is speeding down the street toward the ball, and a nightmare situation begins to unfold.

Despite many previous warnings to stay out of the street,

the daughter runs toward the ball. Just in the nick of time, the father screams: "*Stop!*" Upon hearing her father's voice, the daughter freezes and does just as he says. The command in her father's voice stops her, and she turns to him with fear in her eyes. The father then calls the daughter to him. He hugs her and casts out the fear because of his deep affection for her. When the truck blows by seconds later, the daughter begins to understand why her father shouted at her.

Without such fear, her life would have been in great peril. Because of that fear, the father was able to protect his daughter, and her life was saved. The sound of the father's voice caused her to stop in time to avoid danger. She continued her relationship with her father, and it went even deeper.

At the heart of the father's scream was a fierce, protective love. The scream startled and scared the girl, making her fear him in the moment, but that fear was not to harm her. The fear actually saved her life! Her fear may have come from a lack of understanding in the moment. *Why is Daddy yelling at me for getting the ball out of the street?* she may have wondered. But as the truck sped by and she realized what he did, the fear gave way to a deep and wonderful revelation. Her father had protected her from a horrible danger she couldn't see. What started in fear ended in wonderful love.

When it comes to us and God, we are like the father and daughter. We are God's children. When we see God correctly, we'll carry an appropriate fear which will perpetually turn us toward God and keep us wisely aligned with Him. We will be like the daughter in the story. When we fear God, it will motivate us to love and please Him. James Richards put it best, "The fear of God the Bible encourages is the fear or concern that we may break God's heart!"

Consider this insight from the apostle John who was arguably Jesus' best friend on earth: "There is no fear in love. But perfect love drives out fear, because fear has to do with punishment. The one who fears is not made perfect in love" (1 John 4:18 NIV).

The right kind of fear that wisdom brings will give us an accurate picture of God and posture toward Him, keeping us from offending Him and endangering ourselves with sin. When we carry an accurate view of the fear of the Lord, we gain a stronger relationship with God. And we find wisdom.

Abundant Life

The fear of the Lord leads to wisdom, and wisdom leads to an abundant life that can only be found in a relationship with Jesus. There are so many blessings that come to us when we fear God:

- The fear of God leads to *repentance*.
- The fear of God leads to *knowledge*.
- The fear of God leads to *obedience*.
- The fear of God leads to *peace of heart*.
- The fear of God leads to *longer life*.
- The fear of God leads to *the presence of God*.
- The fear of God leads to *joy*.
- The fear of God leads to *wisdom*!

Wisdom ushers us straight into the heart of God. It brings a life beyond what we can dream, and takes us into an eternity that is like nothing we can experience in this life. Wisdom leads us to eternal life and an incredible existence that never ends.

Chasing Wisdom

> Then I applied myself to the understanding of
> wisdom, and also of madness and folly, but I
> learned that this, too, is a chasing after the wind.
>
> ECCLESIASTES 1:17 NIV

There are a few cautions we do want to give. First, if in your pursuit of wisdom you find yourself wondering why you are even searching for it, you will find that there is a form of wisdom that is misguided. If the wisdom you find does not end with you being more unified with God, then it's the wrong kind of wisdom. There is a worldly wisdom that doesn't lead to God but leads to an unending search for truth. Wisdom that is not rooted in the fear of the Lord is, in the end, foolishness. It is disconnected from God. Solomon says the fear of the Lord ends in the knowledge of God. This is not a head knowledge like something found in a classroom. It's a knowledge of the heart. It's growing a heart of wisdom by walking with Jesus daily.

We have to remember something about wisdom's invitation: we must accept it. A hard truth is that some will learn to fear the Lord, and others will not. There is a word for those who neglect and even reject this fear of the Lord and thus reject wisdom. They are called fools. Or, better put, *we* are called fools because at some point, we have all neglected wisdom, ignored God, and hurt others and ourselves.

Most of us don't choose to be foolish. None of us in our right mind wants to be a fool. We certainly don't make the deliberate choice to ruin our lives and bring pain upon ourselves. But if we want to be wise, we must accept the reality that we can sometimes act like fools. Some will accept wisdom, and others won't. Out of those who don't—some know they are being fools, and others are fools but don't realize it. Unfortunately, foolishness is something we don't see in the mirror.

Wisdom tells us not to judge others and deem them fools but instead to reflect upon our own hearts and lives and look for ways sin might have crept in. Does foolishness lurk in your heart, robbing you of wisdom and all the amazing benefits it offers? When we accept God's invitation and chase wisdom instead of chasing the wind like a fool, our lives will become filled with incredible gifts!

Doing *The Wisdom Challenge* with others has created a brotherhood and made it obvious we need each other to know and grow in wisdom and in the love of God.

BRIAN, PROVERBS PARTNER

Chapter 4

WISDOM'S GIFT

As iron sharpens iron,
so one person sharpens another.
PROVERBS 27:17 NIV

I, Ron, had a serious conflict with a colleague at work. Our relationship got turned sideways, and our trust was broken. I felt the impact of the conflict daily, and it made work miserable. Distrust was destroying my quality of life. In a desperate move, I asked this colleague, who was also a follower of Christ, to do *The Wisdom Challenge*. We both committed to sit at the feet of Jesus and receive the wisdom He had for each of us.

That month was nothing short of miraculous. God did a mighty work in our lives as we daily shared what God was revealing to us. By the time it was over, our working relationship was restored. To this day, though we've since moved on from our previous jobs, we have regular and enthusiastic contact with each other.

Because he understood wisdom's gift, Solomon tells us that whatever we do, get wisdom. Not only is living with wisdom a gift, but a wise life leads to many blessings.

> Get wisdom, get understanding;
>> do not forget my words or turn away from them.
> The beginning of wisdom is this: Get wisdom.
>> Though it cost all you have, get understanding.

Proverbs 4:5, 7 niv

Repetition means emphasis. In these two verses, one word is repeated four times: Get! Get! Get! Get! Get wisdom! This is what *The Wisdom Challenge* is all about. Pursuing wisdom, getting wisdom, is our number one priority. That's why it's also step one in the challenge.

We think it is divine that the thirty-one chapters of Proverbs match the thirty-one days of most months. To get through all of Proverbs in months that don't have thirty-one days, double up on the 30th. In February, you could do two chapters each on the last three days.

Remember what we said about wisdom's impact? You must walk *with* the wise to become wise. *The Wisdom Challenge* isn't an exercise for you to read Proverbs alone. It's a challenge to read it *with* someone and share what God's teaching you through it. Sure, you can find wisdom by going through Proverbs alone. But you will find *more* wisdom by traveling through it with others. This brings more insight. It brings more motivation. It brings more discipline. And it brings a better result.

The second step is inviting a Proverbs Partner into your wisdom pursuit. Over the years, we have taken *The Wisdom Challenge* with hundreds of other people, and those people have turned around and done the challenge with thousands more. A key theme always runs through each person's story when they share how they chose a Proverbs Partner: God puts people on hearts.

If you're going to do *The Wisdom Challenge*, you'll need a Proverbs Partner. How do you find one? The same way you find wisdom: ask God! Also, ask yourself, *Whose life would I like to enhance with the gift of wisdom?* This could be anyone you have a relationship with. Here's a list of people we've taken the challenge with:

- Spouses
- Children
- Siblings
- In-laws
- Long-time friends
- Classmates
- Colleagues and clients at work
- Neighbors
- Teammates

We recommend finding a time and space to be silent. Quiet your heart and mind from the noise. Ask God who should be your first Proverbs Partner. Be aware of the person or people who come to mind. Could this be who God is nudging you to ask? Typically, a person will quickly come to mind, or a person will keep coming up over and over throughout a few days. This is a good sign God wants you to ask that person to become your Proverbs Partner.

Now you might be thinking, *I'm not sure I have enough wisdom to give to anyone.* Honestly, we both had the same concern. Even after all these years of pursuing wisdom, we are keenly aware that our own wisdom is finite. In fact, we shudder to think that people might make the mistake of considering us some sort of wisdom storehouse because we wrote this book. That's not the way wisdom works. Our goal is not to share *our* wisdom. Our goal is to share *God's* wisdom and encourage you to seek it out for yourself. Solomon offered a supply of the wisdom he received from God, and it became the book of Proverbs. We believe God intends for us to do the same and share the supply of wisdom we receive when we ask for it.

Inviting a Proverbs Partner

Once you have identified the person you'd like to share *The Wisdom Challenge* with, make the invitation. The ask is simple: you're inviting them to read Proverbs with you, the same chapter on the same day, and then share one verse that jumped out and an insight God gave you.

Most often, we experience *The Wisdom Challenge* by

texting, but it can also be done via email or phone. In the interest of simplicity, we highly recommend keeping the reflection about your one verse very brief, under twenty-five words, so you don't burn out or become overwhelmed. The shorter the daily messages the better since you'll be forming a new habit to continue for at least thirty-one days and beyond.

Your invitation to your Proverbs Partner can go something like this—or share *exactly* this if you want:

> I've discovered a rich experience that I'd like to
> invite you to join me in. It's called *The Wisdom
> Challenge*. It's the pursuit of wisdom together
> through a daily reading of a chapter from the
> book of Proverbs. It's quite simple and takes
> less than ten minutes. It works like this: on our
> own we each read the chapter of Proverbs that
> matches the date—and then we share with each
> other by text (or email) the verse that God seems
> to most highlight to us and a very brief personal
> reflection on it. By the end of the month, we've
> read the book, and we'll be wiser for it!

If they accept your invitation, you're ready to go. If they don't, that's OK! Ask God to put someone else on your heart. Trust us, eventually someone will say yes. Someone will seek wisdom with you because they'll see the value. In our experience, more than 90 percent of those we've invited to join us have accepted.

Once you have your Proverbs Partner, all you will need is access to the book of Proverbs and a way to share. Since we most often use texting to do *The Wisdom Challenge*, we find it convenient to read the daily Proverb with a Bible app on our phones and copy a verse into the message. This makes it fast and easy.

We've also taken *The Wisdom Challenge* the "old school" way, using a bound Bible to look up Scripture (we love this too!). Sometimes instead of retyping the verse, we take a photo of it and text the picture. If this is you and you'd prefer not to use a Bible app to do *The Wisdom Challenge*, make sure to check out chapter 7. We've designed this book to be a companion tool for your challenge and have included space in the back where you can record your daily insights.

Wisdom Multipled

The Wisdom Challenge is an ongoing commitment to continue pursuing wisdom through Proverbs with at least one other person each month. As you see wisdom multiplied, not only will your life be richer, but you will also see wisdom's ultimate gift: it branches out and changes the lives of countless others. You'll watch wisdom pass from one person to another. A common response from our Proverbs Partners after we share a month together is an enthusiastic, "Thank you! I can't wait to do it with… ."

> The mutual encouragement, the accountability, the simplicity, the personal reflections, and the opportunity to experience the knowledge of the Holy One with a brother and friend all were parts of the practical blessings of the thirty-one-day journey through the book of Proverbs.
>
> JARVIS, PROVERBS PARTNER

Chapter 5

WISDOM'S TREE

The fruit of the righteous is a tree of life,
and the one who is wise saves lives.
PROVERBS 11:30 NIV

Wisdom isn't designed to be stored and hidden; it's designed
to be shared. Just like Jesus calls us to be like lights on a hill,
the wisdom He gives us will shine brightly. When we catch
the vision and receive God's gift of wisdom, we desire to pass
it along to others, and challenge them to pass it along to still
others. Wisdom from God multiplies!

Passing Wisdom On

If you were given an unlimited stack of $100 bills and told you could freely give one away each month for the rest of your life to carefully chosen recipients, who would you choose? Imagine how you would feel! We bet it would feel thrilling. Exhilarating. Not only did you receive an incredible gift, but now you're in a powerful position to bless others.

Based on what we've experienced through *The Wisdom Challenge*, we feel like we're walking around with a stack of $100 bills. We freely distribute wisdom to one person each month. We're giving away one of the most powerful, valuable things on earth. It's thrilling!

We're all familiar with the idea of a pandemic. Do you remember some of the earliest reports and reasoning behind social distancing? When something is highly contagious, it can spread from one person to another and to another to another—sometimes very quickly. Wisdom can spread in a similar way—except we can do it intentionally. When it comes to a novel virus, this kind of passing is harmful. But when it comes to wisdom, sharing is very good. In fact, it's world changing!

Wisdom isn't for us to keep to ourselves and isolate. That's not like God. In God's infinite and ultimate wisdom, we're encouraged to give our wisdom away, at no cost, to as many people as we can. Investing our wisdom into others is a sign we love God and others.

Over the last decade, we've both practiced this custom of trekking through Proverbs with a Proverbs Partner month after month. We've invited hundreds of others into this adventure as part of the third step: passing on wisdom. Those partners have in turn invited thousands of others into *The Wisdom Challenge*. Over time, we've watched a contagious spread of wisdom unfold. We call this our "Wisdom Tree."

Planting Trees

After Ron invited me into *The Wisdom Challenge*, around Day 20, he asked me to begin praying about someone to do the challenge with in the coming month. He explained the vision wasn't a one-time thing but an ongoing, daily habit that would keep wisdom going around the world. I prayed about it, and

God put my son, Elijah, on my heart. Just like the first month with Ron, month two was incredible! I looked forward to hearing from Elijah every day. Although we were technically reading the same verses Ron and I read and shared the month prior, it was like a whole new experience. Not only did new things pop out at me, but I got to know my son better. It was like getting a peek into his soul, as if I had a front row seat to how God was working in his life. I loved it!

I have now taken *The Wisdom Challenge* with so many people including my wife, kids, sons-in-law, many FCA staff (from dozens of countries like Ukraine, Ghana, and Korea), friends, athletes, coaches, business executives, and non-profit leaders. In turn, they have done the challenge with hundreds of others—including some pretty impressive people, even an MVP of the World Series!

The most exciting thing to us about *The Wisdom Challenge* is that you never know how God is going to use it to impact people you know and even those you don't know. This simple but powerful concept has exponential impact. The people who accept your invitation are part of your Wisdom Tree, and the people they invite to join them are also on your Wisdom

Tree. We will only know about and see a fraction of the impact we will have made through our Wisdom Trees on this side of heaven. But one day, we will see our entire Wisdom Tree as we face God in heaven. We are fine waiting to see that until our final days come. In the meantime, we both keep watering and growing our trees, trusting God to produce much fruit.

Life Purpose

When I think about those who have shared the journey of getting wisdom with me over the years, the list is similar to Dan's. I've taken this challenge with my wife and kids (many times), authors, comedians, CEOs, business competitors, clients and colleagues, fellow church members, mentors, politicians, filmmakers, entrepreneurs, missionaries, military officers, athletes, and more.

I keep a growing list of over fifty people God has highlighted to me whom I'd like to invite to join me as a Proverbs Partner in the future. I've taken *The Wisdom Challenge* over one hundred times, but it never gets old. My dream is to do *The Wisdom Challenge* five hundred times, which will take me well past the age of ninety. Wisdom enhances our years, right? I'm going for it!

This goal and journey give me great joy. I've had successes in life and received many gifts, but none greater than wisdom. The charge God put on my life to share wisdom—and to grow a Wisdom Tree—brings immense purpose and fulfillment. I consistently find that people are so grateful for this gift. My Wisdom Tree is one among many, and together we're building a wisdom forest. We invite you to grow your own Wisdom Tree in this forest as well.

When to Multiply

We hope you are catching the vision not only for pursuing wisdom in Proverbs and walking through it *with* a partner but also for passing it on so wisdom gets shared month after month. That is the real challenge—keep it going! Grow *your* Wisdom Tree!

If you're up for this challenge, here's what we've learned. It is beneficial to plant a seed about twenty days into *The Wisdom Challenge* with our Proverbs Partners. Toward the end of each month, after they have tasted the wonder of wisdom for several weeks, we issue the challenge: Take the baton next month. Identify your next Proverbs Partner. Pass it on.

Ultimately we hope people will be inspired to do *The Wisdom Challenge* with at least twelve different people over the course of a year. Trust us, it's doable! We're both busy guys, but once we got a taste of wisdom, we couldn't stop pursuing more. We invite you to join us in this passionate pursuit.

Here is an example of the seed we plant toward the end of a month. We either call, email, or text this:

> If this month-long journey of pursuing wisdom
> through Proverbs has been rich in your own
> heart and life, is there someone you can think of
> that you'd like to bless with the experience next
> month—a relative, a colleague, a neighbor, or a
> friend?

If they're open to doing this and indicate an intention to keep it going, you can send them a message you suggest they use when inviting someone into *The Wisdom Challenge*. Remind them to replicate the approach you took when you invited them to be your Proverbs Partner, and send them this helpful text:

> "I've discovered a rich experience that I'd like to invite you to join me in. It's the pursuit of wisdom together through the daily reading of a chapter from the book of Proverbs. It's quite simple and takes less than ten minutes a day. On our own we each read the chapter of Proverbs that matches the date, and then we share with each other the verse that God seemed to most impress on our hearts and perhaps a very brief reflection on it. By the end of the month we've read the book, and we're wiser for it! Let me know if *The Wisdom Challenge* is of interest, and we can start this together on the first of next month."

Of course, there's no expectation or pressure on you to do this. The month we've been sharing together here has been wonderful and stands by itself as a blessing. But I share the idea of extending the blessing with you as it's been so special for me to do this with others over the months.

Praying God's blessing on you in your continued pursuit of wisdom—and of Him!

Our prayer is that many will receive your invitation to journey through Proverbs with you and accept your challenge to keep it going. When we give others the gift of wisdom, we are leading well. Leadership is caring, loving, and serving others. When we invite them to grow in wisdom, we experience the joy of seeing them transformed by the power of God.

Impacting Thousands

Say you're in! You're committed to growing a Wisdom Tree by passing on wisdom through *The Wisdom Challenge* and encouraging your Proverbs Partners to keep it going each month. We wanted to show you what could happen if just two out of the twelve people you challenged in a year decided to do *The Wisdom Challenge* with twelve others—and then if two out of their twelve people took the challenge and so on.

Within twelve generations, you would have more than twenty-four thousand Proverbs Partners in your Wisdom Tree. Wow!

Generation	Proverbs Partners
1st Generation (You)	12
2nd Generation	24
3rd Generation	48
4th Generation	96
5th Generation	192
6th Generation	384
7th Generation	768
8th Generation	1,536
9th Generation	3,072
10th Generation	6,144
11th Generation	12,288
12th Generation	24,576

Giving the gift of wisdom to a dozen others in a year is quite significant. But if you are intentional and carefully challenge others to pass the torch, you just might build a Wisdom Tree with thousands or tens of thousands of others. Imagine the stories from your Wisdom Tree that will be told as a result of God's Word transforming lives through your life and obedience to pursue wisdom.

Marriages restored.

Relationships reconciled.

Families reunited.

Faith renewed.

Disciplines reignited.

Dreams realized.

Addictions removed.

Who do you hope to see on your Wisdom Tree? Can you imagine it: thousands of lives forever changed because you committed yourself to obtaining wisdom? If we all invited just one person each month into a wisdom journey, and they did the same, we would witness millions of lives changed by the power of God. We would watch wisdom transform the world. Now that's a legacy worth pursuing!

> Going through *The Wisdom Challenge* with Ron has changed my life. Over the last seven years, over three thousand people are now pursuing wisdom, including those I have shared the challenge with directly or who have heard about it from those I've challenged.
>
> KEVIN, PROVERBS PARTNER

Chapter 6

WISDOM'S LEGACY

All go to the same place;
all come from dust,
and to dust all return.
ECCLESIASTES 3:20 NIV

In 1888, Alfred Nobel was mourning the loss of his brother Ludvig when his grief was magnified. He'd just read the obituary in a French newspaper, but it wasn't his brother's…it was his! An editor had confused the brothers and wrote this headline, "The Merchant of Death Is Dead."

Alfred Nobel's accidental obituary described him as a

man who got rich by helping people kill one another; after all, he was the inventor and producer of dynamite. Shaken by this appraisal of his life, Nobel resolved to use his wealth to change his legacy. When he died eight years later, he left more than $9 million to fund awards for people whose work benefited humanity.

We know these awards as Nobel Prizes. Alfred Nobel had a rare opportunity—to look at the assessment of his life at its end and still have the chance to change it. Before his life was over, Nobel made sure to invest his wealth in something of lasting value. He finished well. More importantly, he changed his legacy and the legacy of others. Because he didn't want to be known as the "The Merchant of Death," Nobel chose to rewrite his story as "The Founder of the Nobel Peace Prize." And that story became his legacy.

Today Not Tomorrow

Legacy starts today not tomorrow. The decisions and choices we make today determine the stories people will tell about us tomorrow. In the movie *Dead Poets Society,* there is a scene where the teacher played by Robin Williams confronts his students with the fact they will all soon be "food for worms." He encourages them to look closely at the old photos of the athletes in the trophy case, and he says, "They have all become fertilizer for daffodils." The teacher goes on to say, "*Carpe diem*! Seize the day!"

Solomon spoke this same message three thousand years earlier when he said, "All go to the same place; all come from dust, and to dust all return." Solomon wrote this not to depress his readers for centuries to come, but because through his wisdom he understood what great literature tries to tell us: appreciate today.

We will all face the end of life; we will eventually return to dust. We're not mentioning this to depress you but to encourage you with the timeless challenge. Seize the day! Don't put this book on a shelf and think, *I'll get to it later*. Even if it's in the middle of the month, you can start *The Wisdom Challenge now*. Don't wait!

We're issuing this exciting challenge because it comes with a genuine opportunity to make a mark that far exceeds what *Dead Poets Society* portrayed. Seizing the day means we make every day count. By making every day count, we build a legacy, not just for now but for eternity. Every choice and decision becomes a sentence, paragraph, or chapter to the story that will be told about our lives both on earth and in heaven. Let's take up the charge of wisdom today.

Being able to seize the day, to take action today and not wait for tomorrow, is actually a sign of wisdom. Wisdom makes us aware of our timeline, and it reminds us nothing lasts forever. This is behind a lot of Solomon's writings. Our short lives here on earth come with an opportunity to make an impact both on earth and in heaven. Wisdom says make your life count!

Two Focus Points

Life is not really about leaving a legacy but rather knowing what kind of legacy we're leaving because everybody leaves a legacy. *Legacy is what you leave behind that lives on in others.*

As we grow in wisdom, we will undoubtedly become aware that our lives are leaving an impact everywhere we go. It will also create inside of us a goal of leaving a legacy that outlasts ourselves. To build that kind of legacy, one drenched in the wisdom of God, we need to once again follow in Solomon's footsteps and be aware of both a vertical and horizontal focus. Look at Ecclesiastes 3:11: "He has made everything beautiful in its time. He has also set eternity in the human heart" (NIV).

A vertical focus connects our pursuit of wisdom to God. This is vital in having a relationship with God. When we take our eyes off ourselves and others, we can fix our eyes on Jesus, who is the author of our faith and the source of wisdom.

> Fixing our eyes on Jesus, the pioneer and
> perfecter of faith. For the joy set before him he
> endured the cross, scorning its shame, and sat
> down at the right hand of the throne of God.

> HEBREWS 12:2 NIV

Leaving a legacy of wisdom requires that our lives maintain a vertical focus that is all about a personal, passionate relationship with Jesus Christ. As we grow in our walk with Him, we increase our wisdom, and we will tend to focus on the things that matter most—eternal things. Wisdom won't be something we strive for but the foundation from which we live.

So we fix our eyes not on what is seen, but on
what is unseen, since what is seen is temporary,
but what is unseen is eternal.

2 CORINTHIANS 4:18 NIV

Think about it this way: God's wisdom leads to a life that never ends. Wisdom leads to unity with God, forgiveness for sins, resurrection from the dead, and life in the presence of God that never ends. No wonder Solomon says, "Get wisdom!"

Not only does leaving a legacy full of wisdom require a vertical focus, but we must live with a horizontal focus too. A horizontal focus means we connect our pursuit of wisdom to people. We aren't merely concerned with our own lives but also with the lives of others.

Legacy is not about you. Let that sink in. Too often we focus on *our* legacy—we think legacy is about us. The irony of legacy is that it's about making a difference for others. It's what you give, not what you get. It's what you leave that lives on in the lives of others. *The Wisdom Challenge* is about the opportunity to deposit wisdom into the lives of countless others, not to build and puff yourself up. *Legacy is all about people.*

A horizontal focus means we get our eyes off ourselves and consider others. It's walking with someone else. It's investing today, seizing the day, not just for our own gain but to see others benefit and grow too. When we make the pursuit of God's wisdom our highest priority, we will impact those around us. When we catch a vision for sharing wisdom with many others who in turn will share it with hundreds or even thousands of others, we leave a legacy.

Leaving a Legacy

The opportunity to leave a legacy of wisdom is before you. It's the same opportunity that God put before us several years ago, and we've since run with it. Part of that legacy now includes you. We hope you'll take hold of it and catch this vision. It's incredible!

The Bible says the wise will take hold of the opportunity of wisdom and it will reverberate with an unbelievable return throughout eternity. Wisdom leads us straight to God and unity with Him forever.

If you look for it as for silver

>and search for it as for hidden treasure,

then you will understand the fear of the LORD

>and find the knowledge of God.

PROVERBS 2:4–5 NIV

You have the opportunity to define and refine your legacy by taking *The Wisdom Challenge*. As you consider diving in, remember that it's a priceless gem. Wisdom is more valuable than anything. It's most certainly worthy of ten minutes of your day.

We pray you'll add *The Wisdom Challenge* into your daily routine for years to come. We pray your wisdom journey will help bring meaning and purpose to your life—and glory to the God of wisdom. We believe wisdom can have the same impact on you as it's had on us—a positive impact and a big, growing Wisdom Tree.

Today, more than one hundred months, three thousand days, and two hundred Proverbs Partners later, we are still taking *The Wisdom Challenge* every month and every day. We know that the first time we experienced God's invitation to feast on wisdom wasn't just for us. It was for you too. If you are ready to gain wisdom and change your life, we hope you'll accept this invitation.

Choose to make wisdom the heart of your legacy. Choose to be part of multiplying God's wisdom and impacting the lives of countless others. Start with those you know and love and watch God spread it to thousands more. Just watch. Your life will be changed. The world will never be the same. This is wisdom's legacy. It can be your legacy. Take hold of it today.

This journey through Proverbs has reminded me that God speaks through Scripture in fresh ways if we choose to tune in and listen. I enjoyed hearing my family members' thoughts on the same verses I was reading each day. Scripture in the context of community is the way to go, and *The Wisdom Challenge* allows for that!

RANDY, PROVERBS PARTNER

Chapter 7

WISDOM'S JOURNEY

The one who gets wisdom loves life;
the one who cherishes understanding
will soon prosper.
PROVERBS 19:8 NIV

This chapter is designed for you to maximize your journey through Proverbs by capturing your key verse and insight each day. Write them here and text or email a photo to your Proverbs Partner. Encourage your partner to grab a copy of *The Wisdom Challenge* (or give them one!) so you can share the experience.

WISDOM'S JOURNEY:

PROVERBS 1

From all nations people came

to listen to Solomon's wisdom,

sent by all the kings of the world,

who had heard of his wisdom.

1 KINGS 4:34 NIV

My Verse

My Insight

WISDOM'S JOURNEY:
PROVERBS 2

If you want to be a wise person,

you need a Bible.

ALISTAIR BEGG

My Verse

My Insight

WISDOM'S JOURNEY:
PROVERBS 3

Jesus grew in wisdom and stature,

and in favor with God and man.

LUKE 2:52 NIV

My Verse

My Insight

WISDOM'S JOURNEY:
PROVERBS 4

Wisdom is not a product of schooling

but of the lifelong attempt to acquire it.

ALBERT EINSTEIN

My Verse

My Insight

WISDOM'S JOURNEY:

PROVERBS 5

I saw that wisdom is better than folly,

just as light is better than darkness.

ECCLESIASTES 2:13 NIV

My Verse

My Insight

WISDOM'S JOURNEY:
PROVERBS 6

Patience is the companion of wisdom.

My Verse

My Insight

WISDOM'S JOURNEY:
PROVERBS 7

Wisdom is a shelter

as money is a shelter,

but the advantage of knowledge is this:

Wisdom preserves those who have it.

ECCLESIASTES 7:12 NIV

My Verse

My Insight

WISDOM'S JOURNEY:
PROVERBS 8

When the peace of God follows the purity

of God's wisdom into our hearts and lives,

it will affect those around us.

DAVID JEREMIAH

My Verse

My Insight

WISDOM'S JOURNEY:
PROVERBS 9

If any of you lacks wisdom,

you should ask God,

who gives generously to all

without finding fault,

and it will be given to you.

JAMES 1:5 NIV

My Verse

My Insight

WISDOM'S JOURNEY:
PROVERBS 10

A wise owl sat on an oak,

the more he saw the less he spoke,

the less he spoke the more he heard.

Why aren't we like the wise old bird?

UNKNOWN

My Verse

My Insight

WISDOM'S JOURNEY:
PROVERBS 11

All this also comes from the Lord Almighty,

whose plan is wonderful,

whose wisdom is magnificent.

ISAIAH 28:29 NIV

My Verse

My Insight

WISDOM'S JOURNEY:
PROVERBS 12

Wisdom is the right use of knowledge.

CHARLES SPURGEON

My Verse

My Insight

WISDOM'S JOURNEY:
PROVERBS 13

The wisdom that comes from heaven

is first of all pure; then peace-loving,

considerate, submissive,

full of mercy and good fruit,

impartial and sincere.

JAMES 3:17 NIV

My Verse

My Insight

WISDOM'S JOURNEY:
PROVERBS 14

The chief means for attaining wisdom,

and suitable gifts for the ministry,

are the holy Scriptures and prayer.

JOHN NEWTON

My Verse

My Insight

WISDOM'S JOURNEY:
PROVERBS 15

Who is like the wise?

Who knows the explanation of things?

A person's wisdom brightens their face

and changes its hard appearance.

<small>ECCLESIASTES 8:1 NIV</small>

My Verse

My Insight

WISDOM'S JOURNEY:
PROVERBS 16

The fool wanders,

a wise man travels.

THOMAS FULLER

My Verse

My Insight

WISDOM'S JOURNEY:
PROVERBS 17

Wisdom makes one wise person

more powerful than ten rulers in a city.

ECCLESIASTES 7:19 NIV

My Verse

My Insight

WISDOM'S JOURNEY:
PROVERBS 18

The next best thing to being wise oneself

is to live in a circle of those who are.

C. S. LEWIS

My Verse

My Insight

WISDOM'S JOURNEY:

PROVERBS 19

The mouths of the righteous utter wisdom,

and their tongues speak what is just.

PSALM 37:30 NIV

My Verse

My Insight

WISDOM'S JOURNEY:

PROVERBS 20

Knowledge comes,

but wisdom lingers.

ALFRED, LORD TENNYSON

My Verse

My Insight

WISDOM'S JOURNEY:
PROVERBS 21

I will give you words and wisdom

that none of your adversaries

will be able to resist or contradict.

LUKE 21:15 NIV

My Verse

My Insight

WISDOM'S JOURNEY:

PROVERBS 22

Biblical wisdom begins

with a right relationship with the Lord.

WARREN WIERSBE

My Verse

My Insight

WISDOM'S JOURNEY:
PROVERBS 23

Be very careful, then, how you live—

not as unwise but as wise.

EPHESIANS 5:15 NIV

My Verse

My Insight

WISDOM'S JOURNEY:
PROVERBS 24

When truth presents itself,

the wise person sees the light,

takes it in, and makes adjustments.

The fool tries to adjust the truth

so he does not have to adjust to it.

HENRY CLOUD

My Verse

My Insight

WISDOM'S JOURNEY:

PROVERBS 25

Give me wisdom and knowledge,

that I may lead this people,

for who is able to govern

this great people of yours?

2 CHRONICLES 1:10 NIV

My Verse

My Insight

WISDOM'S JOURNEY:

PROVERBS 26

What is strength

without a double share of wisdom?

JOHN MILTON

My Verse

My Insight

WISDOM'S JOURNEY:

PROVERBS 27

Teach us to number our days,

that we may gain a heart of wisdom.

PSALM 90:12 NIV

My Verse

My Insight

WISDOM'S JOURNEY:
PROVERBS 28

Lord, give me the wisdom

to know what's right

and the courage to do what's right—

even when it's hard.

ANDY STANLEY

My Verse

My Insight

WISDOM'S JOURNEY:
PROVERBS 29

How many are your works, Lord!

In wisdom you made them all;

the earth is full of your creatures.

PSALM 104:24 NIV

My Verse

My Insight

WISDOM'S JOURNEY:
PROVERBS 30

The fear of God is the beginning of wisdom,

and they that lack the beginning

have neither middle nor end.

JOHN BUNYAN

My Verse

My Insight

WISDOM'S JOURNEY:
PROVERBS 31

It is because of him that you are in Christ Jesus,

who has become for us wisdom from God—

that is, our righteousness, holiness

and redemption.

1 CORINTHIANS 1:30 NIV

My Verse

My Insight

AUTHOR BIOS

DAN BRITTON is a speaker, writer, coach, and trainer whose mission is to help people pursue their passion. He serves as the Chief Field Officer with the Fellowship of Christian Athletes where he has been on staff since 1990. Dan travels extensively around the world training thousands of leaders in over ninety countries.

Dan played professional lacrosse with the Baltimore Thunder, earning a spot on the All-Star team, and was nominated by his teammates for both the Service and Unsung Hero awards.

Britton has coauthored six books, *One Word*, *One Word for Kids*, *Life Word*, *Wisdom Walks*, *True Competitor*, and *Called to Greatness*. Additionally, he has authored and edited twelve books with the Fellowship of Christian Athletes.

Dan is a frequent speaker for companies, nonprofits, sports teams, schools, and churches. He has been interviewed by national outlets like FOX News, CBS News, and Fast Company. He still plays and coaches lacrosse and enjoys running marathons, even completing the Boston Marathon twice.

Dan and his wife, Dawn, reside in Overland Park, Kansas, and have three adult children: Kallie, Abby, and Elijah.

Email Dan at dan@fca.org and
follow him on social @fcadan.

RON FORSETH is a business strategist, writer, marketer, mentor, and ultra-distance walker. His mission in life is to acquire, apply, and multiply abundant wisdom to make a better eternity for himself, his family, and millions of others. He has trained teachers and business leaders across Asia and America and has lived in many cities and countries including Mexico, China, Hong Kong, and Mongolia.

Ron has a Bachelor of Arts in political science and a Master of Arts in English from Colorado State and has done graduate work at Seattle Pacific, UT Arlington, and University of Oregon.

For over ten years, Ron served as vice president for Business Development for Outreach, Inc. and was concurrently general manager of Outreach Media Group, Outreach Web Properties, and director of advertising for *Outreach* magazine. He is the founding executive editor of ChurchLeaders.com and long-time general manager of SermonCentral.com, the world's largest online community of pastors.

Forseth has served as lead ambassador for Westfall Gold, a major donor consultancy that has raised over $1 billion for nonprofits. He is president/CEO of the business strategy firm Forseth Development, Inc. and founder of The Wisdom Society.

Ron and his wife, Carol, reside in Colorado Springs, Colorado and have two adult children: Rachel and Randy.

Email Ron at ron@wisdomchallenge.com
and follow him on social @ronforseth.

NEXT STEPS

Visit WisdomChallenge.com

On this site you will find these resources
for pursuing wisdom for a lifetime:

- Free tools for building **Your Wisdom Tree**
- Invitation templates for *The Wisdom Challenge*
- Information about free membership in
  The Wisdom Society
- Free registration to **The Wisdom Seminar**
- More free tools and resources for **Growing in Wisdom**

Grow in wisdom and share it with others at

WisdomChallenge.com
Facebook.com/WisdomChallenge